maze adventure

ARCTURUS

ARCTURUS

This edition published in 2013 by Arcturus Publishing Limited
26/27 Bickels Yard, 151–153 Bermondsey Street,
London SE1 3HA

Illustrated by Andy Peters
Designed by Trudi Webb
Written by Lisa Regan
Edited by Samantha Noonan

ISBN: 978-1-78212-291-3
CH002726EN
Supplier 05, Date 0813, Print Run 2538

Printed in Singapore

Contents

EUROPE 6

AFRICA 26

SOUTH AMERICA 38

NORTH AMERICA 54

ASIA 80

AUSTRALASIA 98

ANSWERS 116

Are you ready... for the adventure of a lifetime?

Join us, Max, Millie and our pet dog, Mojo, on a round-the-world trip to see all the most amazing and exciting sights the planet has to offer! Everywhere we go, we will need your help to solve the tricky mazes, find hidden objects and learn some fascinating facts! We're going to take lots of photographs and make notes along the way.

The world's a pretty big place, so we'd better get started!

NORTH AMERICA

SOUTH AMERICA

Welcome to EUROPE

We're so excited! Our adventure starts in Northern Europe, high up in Finland in the Arctic circle. From there, we're heading, or maybe even sledding, down to chilly Norway. Then we hope to hop across to the volcanoes of Iceland to warm up! From there, we're taking in some history in London, UK, and calling at the famous Berlin Zoo in Germany. There's more sightseeing and history at the Eiffel Tower in Paris and farther south in two of Italy's most famous cities, majestic Rome and watery Venice. Finally, we're visiting Athens in Greece, to see the amazing ruins and learn all about the ancient Greeks!

START

FINLAND

ICELAND

SWEDEN

NORWAY

ESTONIA

LATVIA

LITHUANIA

DENMARK

BELARUS

UNITED
KINGDOM

IRELAND

POLAND

GERMANY

UKRAINE

SLOVAKIA

AUSTRIA

HUNGARY

FRANCE

ROMANIA

SERBIA

BULGARIA

SPAIN

FINISH

PORTUGAL

ITALY

GREECE

Arctic Adventure

We are trekking across the frozen Arctic, at the far north of the planet. The scenery is beautiful, but covered in snow and ice, with only a few creatures brave enough to live here. Brrrr!

FACT FILE

COUNTRY: Finland
CONTINENT: Europe
CAPITAL CITY: Helsinki

The Arctic is not a country in itself, but contains parts of eight countries, including Russia, Canada, USA, Finland and Iceland. The top part of Finland, including the region of Lapland, is inside the Arctic Circle. This is the area near the North Pole, where the sun stays in the sky for 24 hours on June 21st. A lot of Finland is flat and covered in lakes, as thick glaciers eroded much of the high land.

Polar bears live in parts of the Arctic.

Walrus – polar bear food!

Find a path through the ice so that Max, Millie and Mojo don't get their sleigh stuck like Santa has!

START

END

DID YOU SPOT?

20 lost Christmas presents

4 seals

the nosy narwhal

a sneaky orca whale

9

Northern Lights

Wow! Today we are visiting Norway to see the Northern Lights. They are totally amazing, swirling patterns of light in the night sky.

FACT FILE

COUNTRY: Norway
CONTINENT: Europe
CAPITAL CITY: Oslo

The Northern Lights are created by electrically charged particles bumping together in the atmosphere. They can often be seen in northern Norway between late autumn and early spring. Norway is in part of Europe called Scandinavia, and stretches from its capital Oslo, in the south, to the far north in the Arctic. Its coastline is packed with stunning fjords: long, narrow valleys with steep sides, created by glaciers.

Some fjords have coral reefs at the bottom!

Reindeer or caribou

Show Max and Millie how to ski through the slopes of the maze to reach the snug log cabin.

START

END

DID YOU SPOT?

4 reindeer

4 snowy owls

3 mountain goats

5 beavers

11

Hot Spot!

We can't wait to explore Iceland... it may be icy in some parts of the country, but it's also a blast because of its many volcanoes!

FACT FILE

COUNTRY: Iceland
CONTINENT: Europe
CAPITAL CITY: Reykjavik

Red hot molten rock called lava erupts from the volcanoes.

Iceland is an island in the far north of Europe, situated in part of the ocean where two tectonic plates meet. These plates are slowly but constantly pulling apart from each other, which leads to a large number of active volcanoes, hot springs and steam seeping out of the ground. Iceland's capital is the most northerly capital in the world, and about half of the people in the whole country live there.

Super-scalding steam

Max, Millie and Mojo need to watch out for the lava flows and hot water if they want to make it safely through the maze.

START

END

DID YOU SPOT?

3 puffins

12 bathers

4 waterspouts

the clump of grass

13

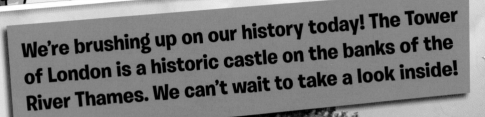

On Guard

We're brushing up on our history today! The Tower of London is a historic castle on the banks of the River Thames. We can't wait to take a look inside!

FACT FILE

COUNTRY: United Kingdom
CONTINENT: Europe
CAPITAL CITY: London

Today, the Tower of London is home to hundreds of precious objects such as crowns, swords, bracelets, rings and royal robes. In past centuries it was a prison and many people, including kings and queens, have been thrown in the dungeons here. The Tower was built as a castle for William the Conqueror after he became King of England in 1066. It has also been used as a royal zoo!

The guards at the Tower wear special uniforms and are nicknamed Beefeaters.

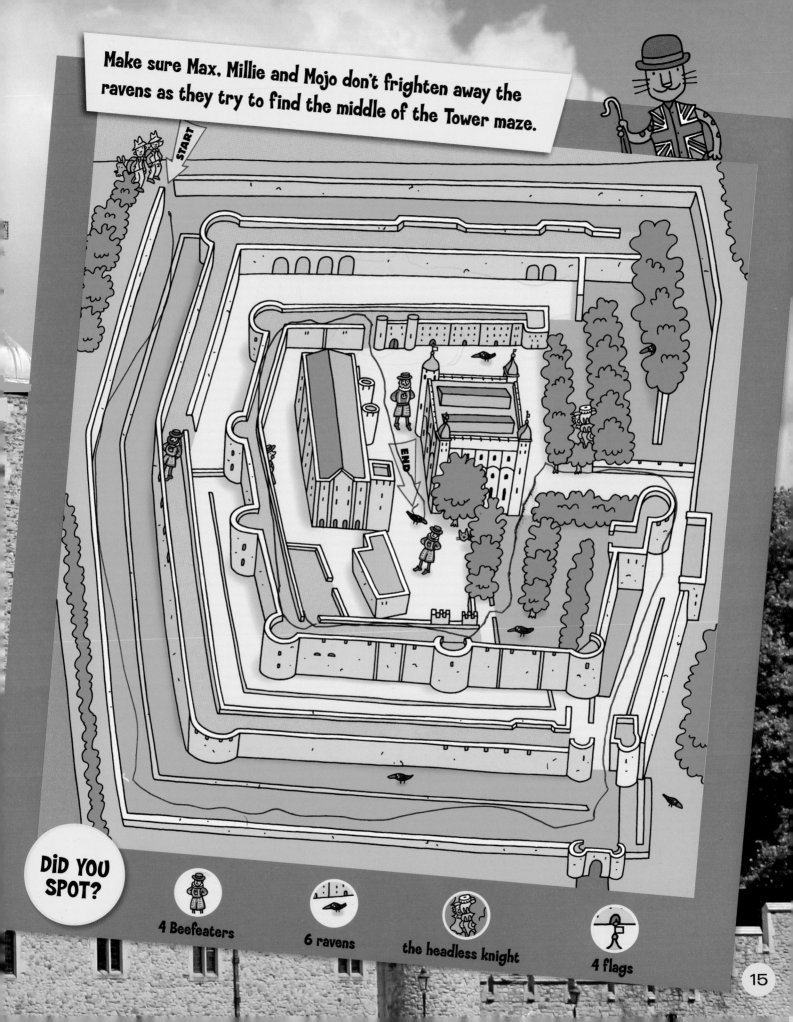

A Day at the Zoo

Berlin Zoo is the oldest zoo in Germany. No dogs are allowed in but Mojo is happy seeing Berlin's other sights while he waits!

Berlin Zoo opened in 1844 but was destroyed during World War II, along with many of Berlin's historic buildings. The impressive Brandenburg Gate (pictured) was damaged, and restored at the start of the 21st century. After World War II Germany was split into two countries, East and West Germany. Berlin was divided for around 30 years by the Berlin Wall, but today it is one busy, thriving, united city.

The Berlin Wall, which divided the city in two, was built in 1961.

Help Max and Millie find a way along the paths, without getting blocked by any of the animals.

START

END

DID YOU SPOT?

3 prickly porcupines

2 busy beavers

the clever chameleon

the crafty croc

17

Bonjour!

We are at one of the most famous sights in the world! The Eiffel Tower in Paris is made of iron and we are taking a lift almost to the top!

FACT FILE

COUNTRY: France
CONTINENT: Europe
CAPITAL CITY: Paris

Grand Palais

The Eiffel Tower was built in 1889 as a dramatic entrance archway for the World's Fair held in Paris. At the time it was the world's tallest structure. It was meant to be pulled down after 20 years, but it was kept standing and has now had more than 250 million visitors! Paris is full of historic sights, such as the Grand Palais, a huge exhibition hall. It is the capital of France, which is the largest country in Western Europe.

The Arc de Triomphe commemorates French soldiers.

Our friends have seen the sights – now they want to come down! Help them to the bottom of the tower.

START

END

DID YOU SPOT?

the UFO

the French poodle

the red balloon

the bunny rabbit

19

Watery World

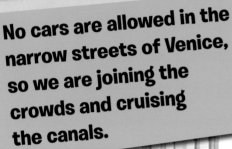

No cars are allowed in the narrow streets of Venice, so we are joining the crowds and cruising the canals.

FACT FILE

COUNTRY: Italy
CONTINENT: Europe
CAPITAL CITY: Rome

Venice is in the north of Italy, and is built on lots of islands in a lagoon. Its buildings crowd along the edges of canals and are held above the water on wooden stilts. The islands are linked by beautiful bridges, and at the edge of the city sits St Mark's Square. The traditional way to get around is on a gondola – a long, narrow boat rowed by a skilled gondolier with a single oar.

Venice is famous for its carnival and masked costumes.

Gondolier here!

Roman Ruins

Our next stop is Rome in Italy, to have some amazing Italian pizza and pasta. Ciao, everyone!

Rome is Italy's largest city and is full of historical sites. In ancient times, it became the centre of an enormous empire called the Roman Empire, which covered huge parts of Africa and Europe. The Colosseum was built between 72 and 81 AD as a giant stadium where around 50,000 people could watch gladiators fighting. Amazingly, it could even be filled with water to show pretend sea battles!

The Trevi Fountain took 30 years to complete.

Can you help Max, Millie and Mojo through the Park of the Monsters in Bomarzo?

START

END

DID YOU SPOT?

6 owls

3 spiders' webs

the hairy beast

2 mysterious monsters

Going for Gold

Join Max, Millie and Mojo in Greece where they are following in the footsteps of ancient rulers, Olympians, and Greek gods.

FACT FILE

COUNTRY: Greece
CONTINENT: Europe
CAPITAL CITY: Athens

Part of the Acropolis

Athens in Greece is one of the oldest cities in the world. It is where the first Olympic games were held, in 776 BC. The ancient Greeks are credited with shaping the civilized world, with great scientists, writers, mathematicians and politicians. The Acropolis is an ancient fortress on a rocky mound overlooking Athens. The city takes its name from Athena, the goddess of wisdom.

The Greek gods were said to live on Mount Olympus.

Help the adventurers climb down from the Acropolis, through the dusty ruins.

START

END

DID YOU SPOT?

5 Grecian urns

3 sacred cats

the Trojan horse

2 golden chariots

Welcome to AFRICA

There's so much to see in Africa! It's the world's second largest continent so we better get a move on. We're starting in Egypt in the far north, to see the ancient wonders of the pyramids and the River Nile. We plan to follow the Nile down to Uganda, where, if we're lucky, we'll get to see gorillas in the wild. Then it's on to Tanzania, where it's all about the wildlife, and Namibia, with sand dunes as well as safaris! Finally, we're staying in South Africa, to see its busy cities and cool coastlines. Maybe we'll even see some sharks! Are you ready for the trip?

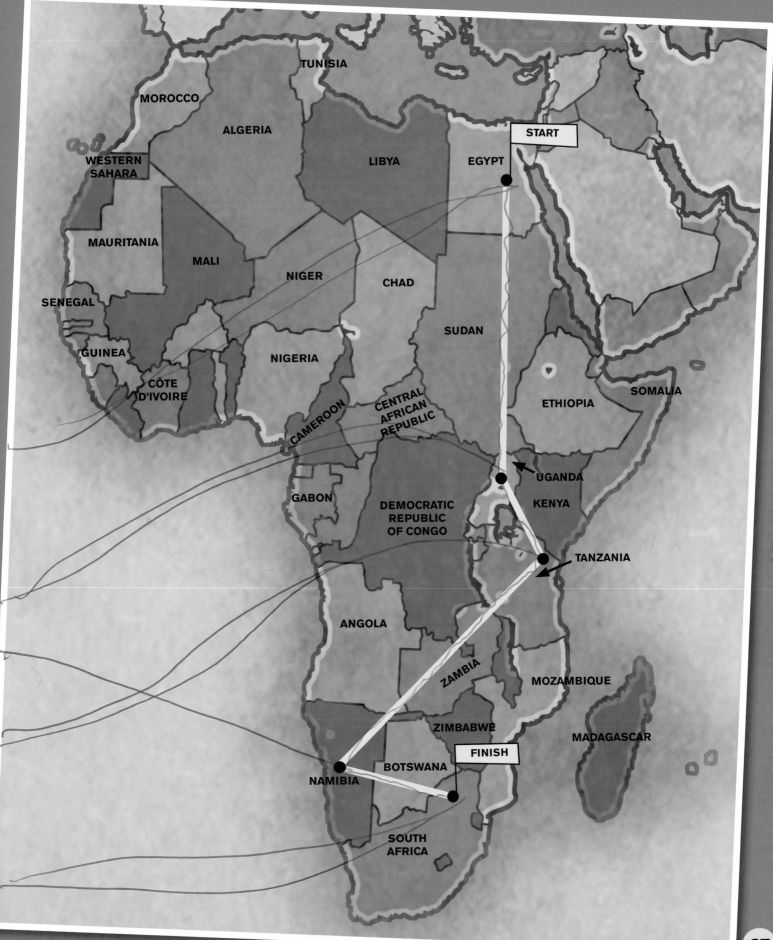

Pyramid Quest

There used to be a list of seven wonders of the Ancient world. Today, the only one left is the Great Pyramid of Giza in Egypt. We can't believe how old it is!

Egypt is an amazing country in the far north of Africa. Large parts of it are desert with extremely high sand dunes. Most people in Egypt live in the narrow Nile Valley where the land is fit for farming and building. The ancient rulers, called pharaohs, built extravagant burial sites along the River Nile. Pharaoh Kufu was buried in the Great Pyramid over 4,500 years ago.

The Sphinx is the world's biggest single-stone statue.

Camel – ship of the desert

The Great Pyramid's smooth white covering no longer exists, so it's a bumpy path to the top these days!

END

START

DID YOU SPOT?

the desert dog   the mischievous mouse   the slithering snake   3 sneaky scorpions

Gorilla Safari

If you want to see the endangered mountain gorilla, the central African rainforest is the place to go. We are trekking through Uganda, hoping catch a glimpse of these mighty mammals.

FACT FILE

COUNTRY: Uganda
CONTINENT: Africa
CAPITAL CITY: Kampala

Some of the world's last remaining mountain gorillas live in the Bwindi Impenetrable Forest in Uganda. The rainforest lies along the edge of the East African rift valley, where the Earth's crust is splitting apart. The River Nile flows north from Lake Victoria, eventually joining the Mediterranean Sea. On its journey, the Nile bursts through a tiny gap in the rocks to form the Murchison Falls (shown in the background) in northern Uganda.

There are only around 700 mountain gorillas left in the wild today.

Shh! Can you work your way through the forest undergrowth without disturbing the sleeping gorillas?

START

END

DID YOU SPOT?

2 okapis

Gerald the giraffe

the sleepiest gorilla

the baby gorilla

Tanzania Trek

We're going on a very long walk! First, we are off to see the wildlife in the national parks, followed by climbing Mount Kilimanjaro, the highest mountain in Africa!

FACT FILE

COUNTRY: Tanzania
CONTINENT: Africa
CAPITAL CITY: Dodoma

Tanzanite is blue but can look violet or reddish-brown under different lights.

Tanzania is on the eastern coast of Africa and its people are mostly farmers, although the country is also Africa's third largest producer of gold. It has its own precious gemstone, tanzanite, found nowhere else in the world. Each year thousands of tourists visit Tanzania's national parks. The Serengeti National Park is home to Africa's Big Five: lions, leopards, elephants, rhinoceros and buffalo.

Before they take on the mountain, the gang are off on safari. Help them on their dusty drive!

START

END

DID YOU SPOT?

4 wary warthogs

3 shy snakes

3 enormous elephants

the sleeping lion

Red Desert

The Namib Desert is so beautiful! The red dunes are caused by iron in the sand. You could almost imagine that you are walking on Mars!

Look! It's an impala

Many of Namibia's sand dunes are pink or orange, but the oldest ones are red, and some of the highest dunes in the world. Namibia is in southern Africa and contains two deserts: the Namib and the Kalahari. It is also home to Etosha National Park, where you can see a variety of wildlife, including giraffes, meerkats and several types of antelope, such as impala.

A group of meerkats is called a mob.

This watering hole is a popular place in the dry season! Find a route through the mass of animals in the water.

START

END

DID YOU SPOT?

3 wallowing warthogs

5 cunning crocs

the swimming snake

12 little birds

Southern Tip

We are down at the southernmost point of Africa: a land of gold, diamonds, busy cities and wonderful wildlife. Let's go!

FACT FILE

COUNTRY: South Africa
CONTINENT: Africa
CAPITAL CITY: Pretoria

There's so much to see in South Africa! It has some of Africa's best-known game reserves, where wild animals roam and hunt but remain protected from poachers. It also has thousands of miles of coastline, with regular visits from sharks, whales and penguins. Its largest cities are Johannesburg, incorporating the famous township of Soweto, and Cape Town, overlooked by the flat-topped Table Mountain.

Cape Town nestles at the foot of Table Mountain.

The trio have been staying at the luxurious Palace of the Lost City Hotel! Help them find their way out of the resort.

END

START

DID YOU SPOT?

5 perky parrots

4 slithery snakes

3 cheeky monkeys

2 slinking leopards

Welcome to SOUTH AMERICA

We start our South American trek by exploring Argentina and then we follow the mighty Andes north to Bolivia. The salt flats there are said to be amazing. We can't visit this continent without seeing Machu Picchu, high in the Peruvian mountains, and while we're in Peru we'll be checking out the bizarre Nazca pictures. Then it's on to Brazil, to party at the Carnival and trek through the Amazon forest. After all that excitement, we're heading to the Galapagos Islands for some quiet time with the animals. Phewee!

Going Deeper

We have arrived in Argentina! Our first stop is at the amazing Cave of the Hands in Patagonia. It's amazing to see the paintings left by people thousands of years ago!

FACT FILE

COUNTRY: Argentina
CONTINENT: South America
CAPITAL CITY: Buenos Aires

Argentina is the eighth-largest country in the world, with a fantastic range of scenery. Patagonia is a mountainous region in the south, containing large ice fields and stunning glaciers (just visible here). The Pampas are farther north and are vast, flat grasslands where cowboys called Gauchos herd cattle. The mighty Andes mountains stretch the length of South America, from Venezuela in the north down to Argentina in the south.

The paintings in the caves were made over 9,000 years ago.

Andean condor

Check out the hand paintings at the entrance to the caves, then find your way underground to the exit.

END

START

DID YOU SPOT?

2 sets of handprints

the vampire bat

the scary monster

41

Salty Scramble

We are standing on the world's largest salt flats in Bolivia. It is absolutely vast and a brilliant bright white!

The landscape here is white because it is covered in a thick layer of salt, left behind when an ancient lake dried up. The valuable parts of the salt can be extracted, especially lithium, which is used in the production of electric batteries. Few living things survive out here; the main plant life is the giant cactus that grows on rocky islands on the salt flats. Flocks of flamingo gather in November to breed on the lakes nearby.

Huge piles of salt

Plankton in the water turns the flamingos pink.

Help Max, Millie and Mojo pick their way across the salty crust. Don't forget your water bottle!

START

END

DID YOU SPOT?

2 wild dogs

4 pink flamingos

the Andean goose

43

Lost City

We are up in the mountains of Peru to see the magnificent Inca city of Machu Picchu. It's so amazing, it has been voted one of the new seven wonders of the world!

FACT FILE

COUNTRY: Peru
CONTINENT: South America
CAPITAL CITY: Lima

The Incas built temples to their sun god Inti.

The Inca city was built high on the mountain of Machu Picchu around 1450, but when the Spanish invaded Peru in the 1500s, the city was abandoned. It was forgotten about, by everyone but the locals, until it was rediscovered in 1911 by an American explorer, Hiram Bingham. The site contains many houses, religious buildings and warehouses, plus cleverly terraced fields to allow farming on the steep mountain slopes.

Find a way through the buildings and down the terraces while the condors circle overhead and watch.

START

END

DID YOU SPOT?

3 condors

4 llamas

the ancient crown

Desert Drawings

We are taking a plane ride over the Nazca desert to see all the amazing drawings in the earth. They are so huge, you can't really appreciate them on the ground.

FACT FILE

COUNTRY: Peru
CONTINENT: South America
CAPITAL CITY: Lima

The ground in the Nazca desert is riddled with astounding pictures, made by removing the red pebbles on the surface to leave the pale earth showing underneath. The designs include shapes and patterns, but also birds, people, monkeys and other animals. They were created around 1,600 years ago by the Nazca people but are still there thanks to the dry, windless climate.

Traditional Peruvian clothes

This picture is of a hummingbird.

46

Follow the lines of the patterns and figures to see if you can help Max guide his friends to the finish.

START

END

DID YOU SPOT?

2 tortoises

the old boot

the armadillo

3 scrubby plants.

Party Time

It's time to celebrate! We are hitting the streets of Rio along with two million other people. It's probably the biggest carnival in the world!

Rio de Janeiro hosts its world famous carnival early each year. It lasts for four days, with street parades, music, and samba dancing where rival groups try to outdance each other. The dancers and musicians wear extravagant costumes and dance or ride through the streets on decorated floats. Rio used to be the capital of Brazil, and is famous for its enormous statue of Christ looking down on the city.

All the dancers wear feathers and sparkles!

Join Max, Millie and Mojo in the street parade! They're on the lion float, but need to work their way out of the crowds.

START

END

DID YOU SPOT?

the fire-eater

3 tambourines

4 trumpets

Rainforest Ramble

We have left the bustling city behind and now we are trekking through the Amazon rainforest, home to the mighty Amazon river. It's full of exciting plants and rare creatures to spot!

FACT FILE

COUNTRY: Brazil
CONTINENT: South America
CAPITAL CITY: Brazilia

The rainforest is a vast jungle that spreads across nine countries, although two thirds of it is in Brazil. Its tropical climate makes it lush and teeming with life. The Amazon River flows through the rainforest. Although it is not the longest river in the world, it contains more water than any other river. It pours vast amounts of fresh water far out into the Atlantic Ocean.

There are 2.5 million types of insect living in the rainforest.

Guide Max, Millie and Mojo through the rainforest and see how much local wildlife you can spot on the way!

START

END

DID YOU SPOT?

3 sneaky snakes

5 cheeky monkeys

the armadillo

2 squawking parrots

51

Island Adventure

We have left the mainland and sailed across the Pacific Ocean to the Galapagos Islands. They are tiny, but home to many amazing and unusual animals.

FACT FILE

COUNTRY: Ecuador
CONTINENT: South America
CAPITAL CITY: Quito

The Galapagos Islands are 1,000 km (600 miles) from South America, but are a part of Ecuador on the mainland. When the scientist Charles Darwin visited in 1835 he was fascinated by the creatures here. Lots of the animals are only found on these islands, including the marine iguana, flightless cormorant, and the Galapagos sea lion. The Galapagos giant tortoise can easily live to be over 100 years old.

Male blue-footed booby birds dance to attract a mate.

Giant tortoise

Help to find a route back to the boat, saying hello to the cool creatures the gang pass on the way.

START

END

DID YOU SPOT?

the giant tortoise

the land iguana

the blue-footed booby

3 flying fish

Welcome to NORTH AMERICA

Huge parts of this continent are covered by Canada and the USA, but we're going to start in Mexico to see its bustling cities and ancient sites. We're state-hopping across the USA, from Florida in the south to Alaska in the far north, with lots of stops in between to see the prairie states, the Rocky Mountains, the Grand Canyon, and Niagara Falls on the Canadian border. We're planning some offshore visits, too, to Bermuda in the Atlantic, and Hawaii, far out in the Pacific Ocean. Plus, we can't stay in the USA without visiting New York City and looking down on the world from a skyscraper!

ALASKA

CANADA

FINISH

HAWAII

UNITED STATES OF
AMERICA

NEW
YORK

BERMUDA
TRIANGLE

START

FLORIDA

MEXICO

DOMINICAN
REPUBLIC

CUBA

GUATEMALA

History Trek

We are in sunny Mexico, a land full of beautiful scenery and amazing history. We are going to visit the stepped pyramids and find out more about the brilliant ancient societies that lived here.

Mexico is a country that mixes historical sites with modern cities and tourist resorts. For many centuries, cultures such as the Toltecs, Aztecs, Mayas and Zapotecs thrived in different parts of the country. The Mayas built beautiful palaces, pyramids and temples for their rulers and gods. Ruins like those at Palenque (pictured) and Chichen Itza attract millions of visitors each year.

Nearly 9 million people live in Mexico City.

Find a way down the steps of the pyramid before night falls and the serpent god or jungle spirit come out to play!

START

END

DID YOU SPOT?

5 cheeky monkeys

2 toucans

the jungle spirit

3 sneaky snakes

Lazy River

We have arrived in Florida, at the southeast tip of the USA. It is the warmest state in the whole country (nicknamed the Sunshine State), but it is often threatened by hurricanes.

Florida is famous for its beaches, such as Daytona and Miami, but also for the island chain known as the Florida Keys. These islands stretch from the tip of the Florida peninsula to Key West, and are famous for their Key lime pie! Inland, the Everglades National Park is a wetland area with a very slow-flowing river and mangrove swamps, inhabited by crocodiles and alligators.

You can see real rockets and launch pads at NASA in Orlando, Florida!

Guide the gang on their airboat through the Everglades to reach the outlet at the top.

END

START

DID YOU SPOT?

14 alligators

4 turtles

2 pelicans

the Florida panther

Ocean Explorers

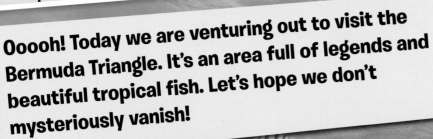

Ooooh! Today we are venturing out to visit the Bermuda Triangle. It's an area full of legends and beautiful tropical fish. Let's hope we don't mysteriously vanish!

FACT FILE

COUNTRY: Bermuda
CONTINENT: North America
CAPITAL CITY: Hamilton

Fishy fun

Angelfish live in the shallow waters around Bermuda

The so-called Bermuda Triangle is a part of the Atlantic Ocean, where boats and aircraft are supposed to have mysteriously disappeared. It stretches from Florida in the west, across to Puerto Rico, and up to the British islands of Bermuda. In fact, this area has no more accidents than any other busy shipping area. Bermuda itself, though, does have many shipwrecks, and its own coral reefs, so it is a diver's paradise.

Watch out for the whirlpools as you navigate through the fabled waters of the Bermuda Triangle!

START

END

DID YOU SPOT?

the UFO

4 sea serpents

the periscope

the unhappy spider

The Big Apple

We are taking in the bright lights of New York City, one of the most famous cities in the world. It is a fantastic mix of people, cuisine and culture from all over the planet!

New York City is the biggest city in the USA, and is nicknamed The Big Apple. It is full of famous sights, including many enormous skyscrapers that stretch high into the clouds. The highest of all is the recently built One World Trade Center. The Statue of Liberty stands at the entrance to New York and was the first thing seen by many immigrants arriving in the country to start a new life.

Catch a yellow cab to get around in the city.

Help the gang climb down the Statue of Liberty from her torch, held high, to the tablet in her left hand.

START

END

DID YOU SPOT?

3 seagulls

4 green birds

the helicopter

the kite

63

Niagara Falls

There are actually three waterfalls at Niagara, which sits on the border between Canada and the USA. We are excited to be in Canada, but Mojo is afraid of the water as it flows so fast.

FACT FILE

COUNTRY: Canada
CONTINENT: North America
CAPITAL CITY: Ottawa

Horseshoe Falls

Passengers on the boat tour get extremely wet!

The largest of the waterfalls is Horseshoe Falls on the Canadian side. It is separated from the American Falls by Goat Island. The third falls, Bridal Veil Falls, are also American. The total water gushing over all three gives them the highest flow rate of any waterfall in the world. Millions of tourists visit each year. The Maid of the Mist boat takes you close enough to the falls to feel the spray!

It is illegal to go over the waterfalls as it is so dangerous, so try it the safe way with this mega maze!

START

END

DID YOU SPOT?

4 purple fish

3 happy ducks

the baby bear

The Maid of the Mist

Tornado Alley

Today, we are in the middle of the USA, in Kansas. It is in the heart of Tornado Alley, where there are often very strong tornadoes.

FACT FILE

COUNTRY: USA
CONTINENT: North America
STATE CAPITAL: Topeka

The Great Plains in Kansas used to be home to large herds of wild bison, North America's biggest mammal. Nowadays bison can only be found in private reserves and national parks. Kansas is famous for tornadoes, violent, swirling columns of air that stretch from the earth to the clouds above. They are also known as twisters. They can cause enormous damage, ripping roofs off houses and sending dangerous debris flying through the air.

Tornado strength is measured from 0-5 on the Fujita Scale.

The explorers are caught up in a twister!
Help them work their way back to solid ground.

START

END

DID YOU SPOT?

3 scared cows

the blue car

the lost bike

the brown bird

67

Cherokee Trail

We are following the Cherokee Trail through Colorado, on the edge of the Great Plains and at the bottom of the mighty Rocky Mountains. Perhaps we will strike gold!

FACT FILE

COUNTRY: USA
CONTINENT: North America
STATE CAPITAL: Denver

The Garden of the Gods contains amazing rock formations.

Colorado is a state made up of mountains, plains, forests and deserts, where several Native American tribes lived or passed through. The Cherokee Trail is named after one such tribe. In 1849, a mixed group of Cherokee and white settlers set off in a wagon train, trekking overland to seek gold in the California hills. Thousands of families rushed to make their fortune, and parts of the path worn by their journeys can still be seen today.

Enjoy the scenery as you wind your way through the foothills of Colorado to find a way from start to finish.

START

END

DID YOU SPOT?

3 grizzly bears

3 giant mosquitoes

the secret railroad

the rattlesnake

Rocky Road

We are at the Grand Canyon in Arizona. This giant valley was carved out of the rock by the Colorado River over millions of years!

FACT FILE

COUNTRY: USA
CONTINENT: North America
STATE CAPITAL: Phoenix

The rock at the base of the Grand Canyon is 1.8 billion years old! Around 5 million people visit each year to gaze at the views, hike around the valley, and admire the many layers of reddish rock that form its steep sides. Arizona also has a gigantic hole made by a meteor crashing into the earth, and the enormous man-made Hoover Dam on its border with Nevada.

Black-tailed prairie dogs live in the Arizona desert.

Help the three friends through the Canyon's rocky paths, and past the winding river, to reach the end.

START

END

DID YOU SPOT?

10 cacti

2 raccoons

the deadly red snake

Cattle Drive

Welcome to cowboy country! We are checking out a cattle drive in Wyoming, then moving on to Yellowstone Park for more explosive adventures!

Wyoming is a large state with lots of land for rearing cattle, and a long history of cowboys who take care of the animals. Yellowstone Park was the world's first national park, and 3 million people visit every year. It is huge and contains canyons, mountain gorges, rivers and lakes, but most famously it has geothermal activity. This produces waterspouts called geysers that squirt boiling water out of the ground.

Old Faithful erupts almost every 90 minutes.

Grazing bison

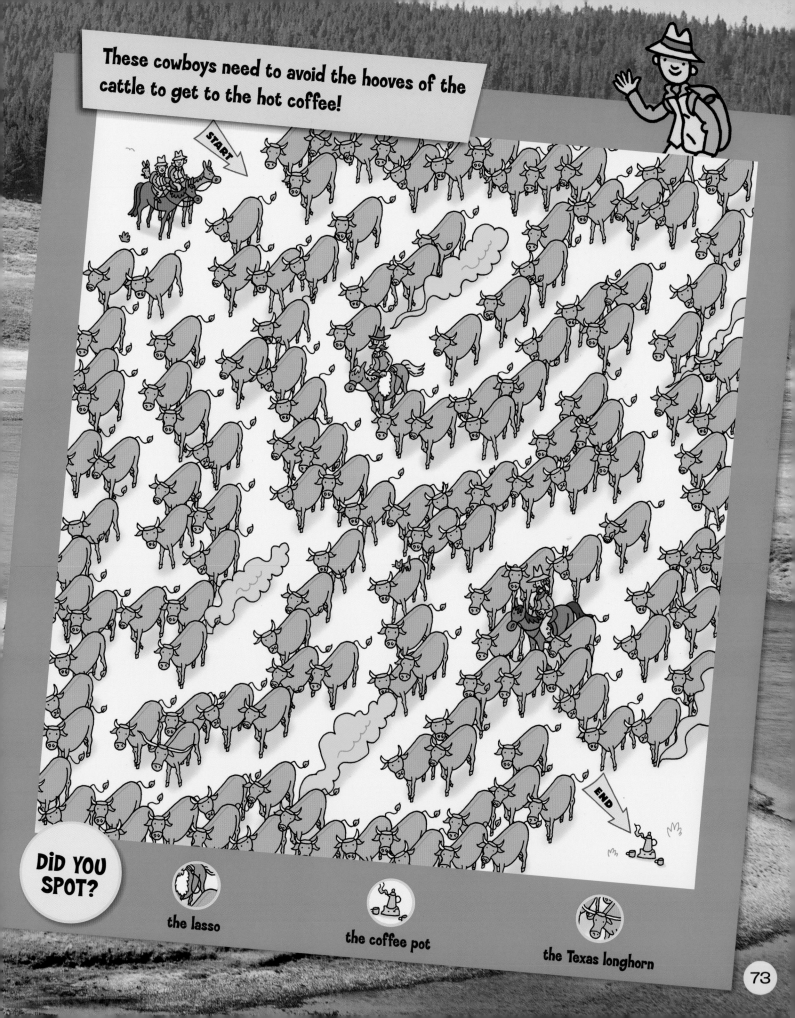

These cowboys need to avoid the hooves of the cattle to get to the hot coffee!

START

END

DID YOU SPOT?

the lasso

the coffee pot

the Texas longhorn

Dinosaur Dig

Next on the trek is Montana, the fourth largest state in the USA, and home of the Glacier National Park and the Dinosaur Trail. We're hoping to see lots of cool fossils!

Rising temperatures make the glaciers smaller each year.

More dinosaurs have been uncovered in Montana than in any other state. There are fossils of all kinds, from the horned Triceratops and huge Apatosaurus to fierce hunters like Deinonychus and T. rex. It's a paleontologist's paradise! The Glacier National Park has ancient wonders, too. There have been glaciers there since an ice age 10,000 years ago.

Take a look at these T. rex teeth!

Can you dig it? Yes you can! Help Max, Millie and Mojo pick their way carefully through the dinosaur remains.

START

END

DID YOU SPOT?

the desert snake

the dino eggs

the hungry mouse

the chisel

The Last Frontier

We're heading for Alaska in the far north. It is huge, wild and sparsely populated – just take a look at that scenery!

FACT FILE

COUNTRY: USA
CONTINENT: North America
STATE CAPITAL: Juneau

Alaska is so large it would cover the 22 smallest states of the USA! It has natural supplies of gas and oil and exports seafood in vast quantities. Alaska has brown bears, grizzlies, black bears, and polar bears in the far north. The brown bears gather by mountain rivers during salmon spawning season, when the tasty fish head upstream to breed, and are easy pickings for the bears.

Alaskan brown bears are bigger than other brown bears.

The White Pass Railroad twists and turns high into the mountains. Can you find a safe route for our friends on the train?

START

END

DID YOU SPOT?

3 brown bears

5 soaring eagles

the grumpy yeti

Island State

Aloha from Hawaii! This tropical paradise was the last state to become part of the USA. It consists of hundreds of islands formed by volcanoes.

FACT FILE

COUNTRY: USA
CONTINENT: North America
STATE CAPITAL: Honolulu

Hawaii grows a third of the pineapples sold around the world!

Hawaii is made entirely of islands in the Pacific Ocean, around 2,000 miles away from the mainland. The 44th US President, Barack Obama, was born in Honolulu on the biggest island, Oahu. One of the world's largest observatories is built on Hawaii's highest mountain, Mauna Kea, where the clear skies and lack of light pollution give excellent results for astronomers.

Take a stroll through the tropical garden and then put your feet up for a nap in the sun.

START

END

DID YOU SPOT?

3 raccoons

2 wily coyotes

5 rats

3 squirrels

Welcome to ASIA

Are you coming with us to Asia? It's the world's largest continent with a huge number of exciting countries to explore. We're starting in the east, in China, with its dragons, temples, busy cities and of course, the Great Wall. From there it's across to the United Arab Emirates on the Arabian Peninsula, and then up we go on a trek to Mount Everest in the massive Himalaya Mountains. When we come back down to earth we'll zoom across to Cambodia, Vietnam and the Philippines, which are watery places, with friendly people and some beautiful religious and historic places to see.

RUSSIA

KAZAKHSTAN

MONGOLIA

START

TURKEY

IRAN

CHINA

JAPAN

IRAQ

PAKISTAN

NEPAL

SAUDI
ARABIA

INDIA

UNITED
ARAB
EMIRATES

FINISH

YEMEN

PHILIPPINES

CAMBODIA

VIETNAM

MALAYSIA

INDONESIA

Dragon Dance

It's time to celebrate! We are in China for the Spring Festival. Teams of dancers carry dragon costumes and perform in the streets to celebrate the arrival of a new year.

FACT FILE

COUNTRY: China
CONTINENT: Asia
CAPITAL CITY: Beijing

China has more people living there than any other country. It is also one of the biggest countries and contains deserts and mountains, subtropical forests and huge grassland areas. The people live mostly in the eastern side of the country. Their New Year celebrations take place in January or February, when small gifts are exchanged and firecrackers are set off to scare away evil spirits.

Red envelopes with money inside bring good luck.

Dancing dragon

Help our friends dance their way through the performers without getting thrown off course.

START

END

DID YOU SPOT?

the dragon with blue eyes

the dragon breathing fire

the dragon who has lost its fire

83

Great Wall

We've taken a trip to the north of China to see the Great Wall, built thousands of years ago to keep out dangerous invaders and control who was allowed into the country.

FACT FILE

COUNTRY: China
CONTINENT: Asia
CAPITAL CITY: Beijing

The Terracotta Army were buried with an ancient Emperor

The Great Wall runs from east to west near the northern border of China. It was built in separate sections for several different emperors. The people who built it were usually criminals, captured enemies and slaves and were not paid. It was constructed over so many centuries that it is a mixture of mud, grass, stone, bricks and wood. The towers were sentry posts and provided shelter and storage.

This should be called the Long and Winding Wall! Try to find a path to the main tower at the end.

START

END

DID YOU SPOT?

5 peeking pandas

2 Chinese dragons

the Ming vase

85

Sight Seeing

China has so many amazing sights, it is hard to know which ones to visit! We're visiting a natural wonder and a man-made structure today.

FACT FILE

COUNTRY: China
CONTINENT: Asia
CAPITAL CITY: Beijing

Buddhism is a popular religion in China, and there are thousands of beautiful Buddhist temples to see. The Shibaozhai Temple (pictured) on the banks of the River Yangtze is built against a rock to keep it upright. The Stone Forest is in the far south of China, and is a landscape filled with natural stone formations that look like trees, as well as animals and people.

Gautama Buddha is the main figure in Buddhism.

Find a way through the strange stone trees to reach the temple in the forest.

START

END

DID YOU SPOT?

3 Chinese dragons

the yellow bird

the giant spider

the lone tree

Man-made Wonders

We are living it up in one of the wealthiest countries in the world, the United Arab Emirates. Time for some sun, sea and luxury shopping!

FACT FILE

COUNTRY: United Arab Emirates
CONTINENT: Asia
CAPITAL CITY: Abu Dhabi

The United Arab Emirates, or UAE, is a country on the Arabian Peninsula next to the Persian Gulf. It is made up of seven emirates. Dubai is famous for its skyscrapers and luxury hotels. The Burj Khalifa skyscraper opened in 2010 as the tallest building in the world. The man-made Palm Islands are also in Dubai, and are shaped like palm trees. They are made from sand pumped from the ocean floor.

The Burj Khalifa contains offices and apartments.

Swim with dolphins in Dubai!

Explore these amazing islands by boating through the channels between them and heading for shore.

START

END

DID YOU SPOT?

the star island

3 crazy crabs

2 sand bunnies

2 periscopes

Head for Heights

We are on top of the world! We are in the Nepalese part of the Himalaya mountain range, which contains eight of the world's ten tallest peaks.

The Himalayan mountain range passes through five countries: Nepal, Bhutan, India, China and Pakistan. It contains the highest mountain in the world, Mount Everest. Climbers can choose whether to start their Everest ascent from North Base Camp in Tibet, part of China, or South Base Camp in Nepal. The beautiful but endangered snow leopard can be found in these mountains.

Yaks often carry supplies for Everest climbers.

Find a way down the snowy slopes for Max, Millie and Mojo. They're following in the footsteps of the mysterious Yeti!

START

END

DID YOU SPOT?

the werewolf

a pair of yeti slippers

the unicorn

3 dead trees

Come to Cambodia

We have made it to Cambodia, a country full of temples and rice fields, with amazing waterfalls and floating villages built on lakes.

The climate of Southeast Asia is perfect for lush tropical rainforests. Many of Cambodia's forests have been chopped down, but the remaining ones are now protected to preserve the plants and animals that live there. The ancient temple at Angkor Wat is the world's largest single religious monument and has been used for both the Hindu and Buddhist faiths.

Stilt houses are safer from floods in the rainy season.

Find a way through the stone surface of the temple from start to finish.

START

END

DID YOU SPOT?

2 giant spiders

the roving rabbit

the temple monkey

the mysterious monster

93

Rainy Season

Next stop, Vietnam, a long, narrow country covered in hills and forests. Like the rest of Southeast Asia, it suffers from heavy seasonal rains called monsoons.

The monsoons don't just hit Vietnam once a year, but twice, in summer and in winter. The nation was isolated from the rest of the world by the Vietnam War (1955–1975), but now has good relations with most countries. During the war, the locals used a lengthy tunnel system for hiding, storage and even for hospital care. These Cu Chi tunnels are now a tourist attraction.

The Indochinese tiger can be found in Vietnam.

Find a way out of the secret tunnels without bumping into the scary giant spiders!

END

START

DID YOU SPOT?

7 scary spiders

8 storm lamps

the cave troll

the secret radio

Ring of Fire

FACT FILE

COUNTRY: Philippines
CONTINENT: Asia
CAPITAL CITY: Manila

We have made it to the Philippines. This country is a string of islands and the proper name for this is an archipelago. The Chocolate Hills (pictured) turn brown in the dry season, like chocolate!

The Philippines are located on the Pacific Ring of Fire, an area in the Pacific where many earthquakes and volcanic eruptions happen. Farmers cut terraces, like large steps, into the sides of slopes to make use of the land. They are watered by an irrigation system from the rainforests high above. The stepped fields keep in the water, instead of it flowing straight to the bottom. Some rice terraces here are 2,000 years old!

Find a path through the rice fields from the top of the slope to the bottom.

START

DID YOU SPOT?

2 watering cans

3 monkeys

the giant spider

END

Welcome to AUSTRALASIA

We ought to be upset, as our journey is nearly finished, but who can be sad when they have the whole of Australasia to see? We're covering a lot of ground to take in the cities, coast, and the hot, dry heart of Australia. Then we're hopping across to Kangaroo Island to check out the wildlife. Next stop is Tasmania, then over the sea to New Zealand. We're staying on the North Island and the South Island as they both have lots of sights and crazy things to do. Fancy a bungee jump, anyone? Finally, we're ending our grand world tour on Kiribati, with an awesome firework celebration. It's so exciting!

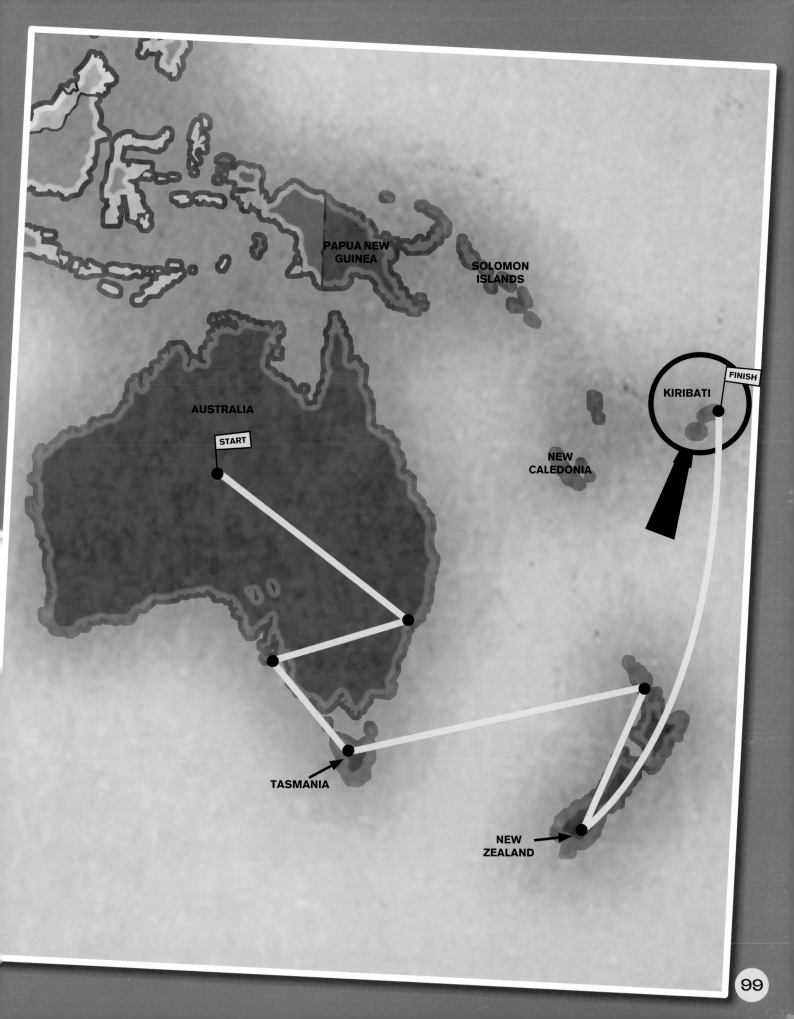

PAPUA NEW
GUINEA

SOLOMON
ISLANDS

KIRIBATI

FINISH

AUSTRALIA

START

NEW
CALEDONIA

TASMANIA

NEW
ZEALAND

Down Under

We are in Australia, a land of extremes. In this one country you can find desert, rainforest, farmlands and even places permanently covered in snow.

FACT FILE

COUNTRY: Australia
CONTINENT: Australasia
STATE CAPITAL: Darwin

Most of the people in Australia live in or near its ten largest cities, mainly around the eastern and southeastern coasts. Canberra was built in 1908 to serve as the country's capital. Inland the terrain becomes drier, rockier and inhospitable. Few people live in these central areas, known as the Bush and the Outback, but there are distinctive landscapes, and animals native only to Australia. These include the red kangaroo, emus, koalas and dingoes.

NEXT
10 km

Uluru is a sacred rock in the middle of Australia.

Go walkabout in the Bush and take a look at the amazing wildlife on your way.

START

END

DID YOU SPOT?

4 snakes

5 wombats

2 wallabies

2 sleeping crocs

City Sights

Welcome to Sydney! It is not Australia's capital but it is the country's largest and oldest city, with friendly people, great beaches and lots to see.

FACT FILE

COUNTRY: Australia
CONTINENT: Australasia
STATE CAPITAL: Sydney

Bondi Beach is a popular tourist spot in Sydney.

One of Sydney's most famous sights is the inspirational Opera House, designed in the 1950s to look like shells sticking out into the water. It contains two main opera halls but about 1,000 rooms altogether. It took six years longer and cost ten times more to build than originally planned! For a different view of the city, you can climb right over the railings of the bridge (pictured) on a guided tour.

Help Max and Millie sing their way through the opera house maze. Mojo is more into howling than singing!

START

END

DID YOU SPOT?

3 opera bunnies

the super soprano

the giant spider

the bemused fish

103

Great Outdoors

The Australian climate lends itself to an outdoor life, especially for the millions of people who live near the coast. We're going to catch some waves!

FACT FILE

COUNTRY: Australia
CONTINENT: Australasia
STATE CAPITAL: Brisbane

The Aussie lifestyle involves lots of swimming, barbecues, outdoor sports and, of course, surfing. Queensland is known as the Sunshine State and its coast is world famous for its beaches, islands and reefs. The Great Barrier Reef is the largest collection of coral reefs on the planet and home to around 400 types of coral, 1,500 species of fish and various large marine wonders such as sharks, turtles and dolphins.

Clownfish live in the anemones of the Great Barrier Reef.

The trio are riding on the crest of a wave with this maze, quite literally! Help them surf safely through it.

START

END

DID YOU SPOT?

2 surfing turtles

4 lurking sharks

4 flying fish

2 steady seagulls

Kangaroo Island

We're going to leave mainland Australia now and explore some of its islands. First stop, Kangaroo Island, off the south coast, across the sea from Adelaide.

This small island is a wildlife haven. If you want to see Australian animals, then come here! It is teeming with kangaroos, koalas and wallabies, but you may also catch a glimpse of something rarer, such as the echidna, which is also sometimes known as a spiny anteater. Don't forget to join in the Kangaroo Island wave, a friendly custom of raising your first finger to any cars that drive past!

Island koalas are causing problems by eating too much.

Help the explorers across the island to their boat in Seal Bay. Hop to it!

START

END

DID YOU SPOT?

4 sneaky sharks

5 cool koalas

4 pleased pelicans

the happy turtle

Tassie Time

Another island hop takes us to Tassie, or Tasmania, an island state at the far south of Australia.

FACT FILE

COUNTRY: Australia
CONTINENT: Australasia
STATE CAPITAL: Hobart

Tasmania is separated from mainland Australia by Bass Strait, which can be crossed by ferry. It has a varied climate, with enough snow in winter to go skiing, and mild summers perfect for swimming or hiking around the magnificent countryside. There are many unusual creatures there, such as the platypus, the wombat and the terrifying Tasmanian Devil (pictured below).

Tasmania is famous for its lavender farms.

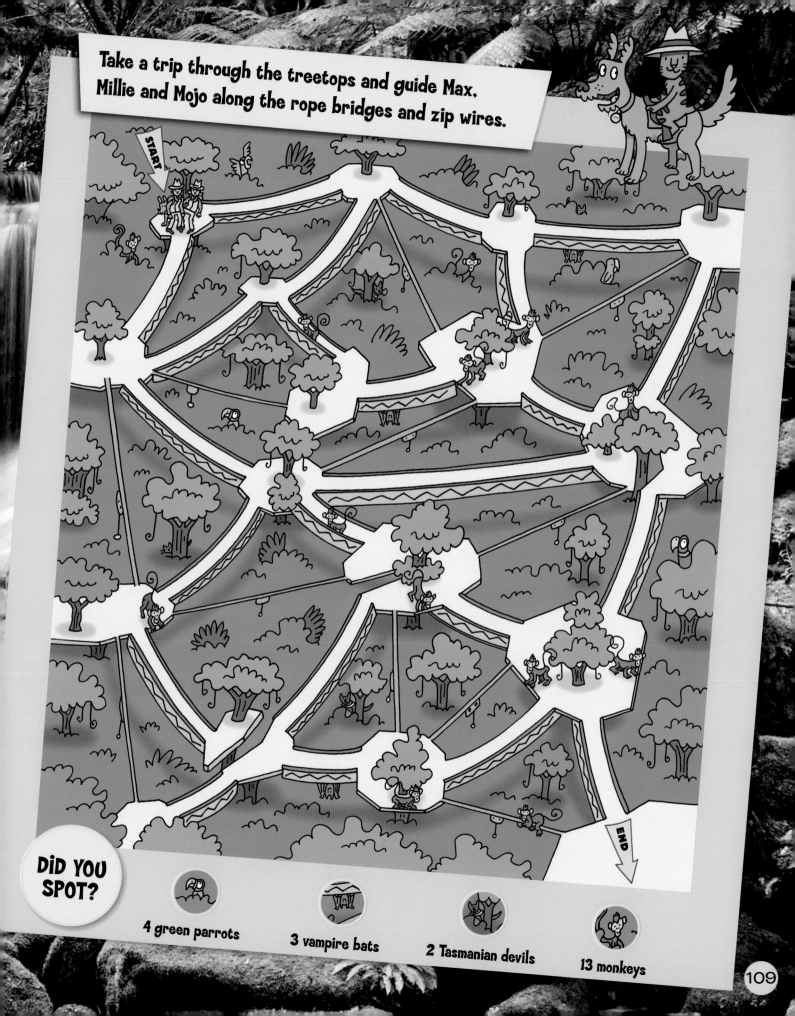

Take a trip through the treetops and guide Max, Millie and Mojo along the rope bridges and zip wires.

START

END

DID YOU SPOT?

4 green parrots

3 vampire bats

2 Tasmanian devils

13 monkeys

Kia Ora!

Which means 'Welcome to New Zealand'! It is so far from other land that it was one of the last places to have humans living there.

FACT FILE

COUNTRY: New Zealand
CONTINENT: Australasia
CAPITAL CITY: Wellington

New Zealand is made up of two main islands, North and South. North Island has the country's capital city, Wellington, and its largest city, Auckland (pictured), home to the Sky Tower. It also has geothermal sites where you can see bubbling mud pools, smell the stinky-egg gases leaking out of the ground, and bathe in the naturally warm waters. The native Maori people still cook food in the steam for tourists to eat.

Chemicals in the water turn the Devil's Bath at Rotorua green.

Fancy a SkyJump? These crazy people are leaping left and right, making a maze for Mojo and his friends.

START

END

DID YOU SPOT?

the giant spider

the shy gorilla

the superhero

3 brown birds

111

Extreme Thrills

Now Max, Millie and Mojo are on New Zealand's South Island. If you're feeling brave, this is the place to show off your daredevil skills.

FACT FILE

COUNTRY: New Zealand
CONTINENT: Australasia
CAPITAL CITY: Wellington

Skydiving is just one way to see the sights!

The mountain scenery on South Island is breathtaking, with glacier-carved lakes, fjords and huge valleys. It has some of the world's largest glaciers, giant rivers of ice that slide slowly downhill, almost to the sea. New Zealand also has a reputation for extreme sports, and there's a huge choice of crazy activities to try, from river rafting and jet boating to bungy jumping, skydiving and canyon swinging!

Help Max climb up the rock face maze to reach Millie and Mojo at the top. Mojo looks rather alarmed up there!

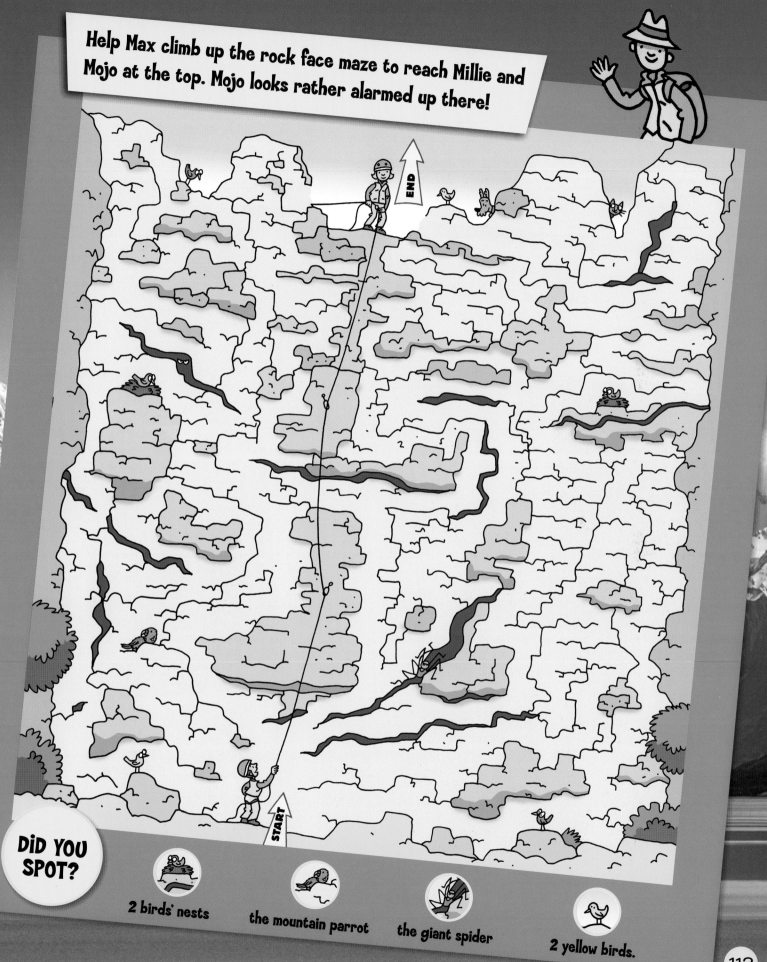

END

START

DID YOU SPOT?

2 birds' nests

the mountain parrot

the giant spider

2 yellow birds.

113

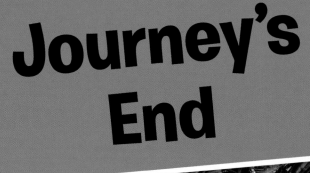

Journey's End

That's it! Max, Millie and Mojo have reached the end of their travels, just in time to join the celebrations in Kiribati.

FACT FILE

COUNTRY: Kiribati
CONTINENT: Australasia
CAPITAL CITY: South Tarawa

Breadfruit is an important crop on the island.

Kiribati is a nation of tiny islands far out in the Pacific Ocean. Most of its islands are coral atolls, which are ring-shaped reefs with a lagoon in the middle. The land is so low that Kiribati may be the first country to disappear because of rising sea levels. Its easterly position on the time zone map means that it is one of the first places to see in each New Year.

The gang have a great view of the New Year's celebrations on Kiribati!

START

END

DID YOU SPOT?

the yellow flower   the green star   the pink elephant   7 red stars

Answers

8-9   **Arctic Adventure**

12-13   **Hot Spot!**

10-11   **Northern Lights**

14-15   **On Guard**

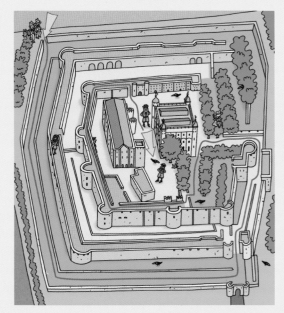

16-17   A Day at the Zoo

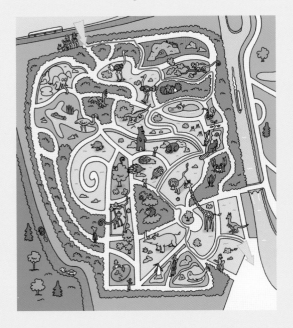

18-19   Bonjour!

20-21   Watery World

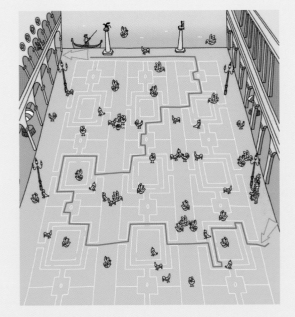

22-23   Roman Ruins

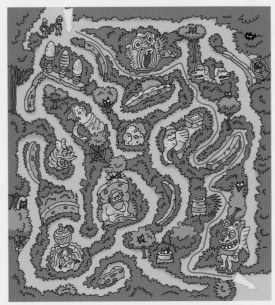

24-25 Going for Gold

30-31 Gorilla Safari

28-29 Pyramid Quest

32-33 Tanzania Trek

34-35 Red Desert

40-41 Going Deeper

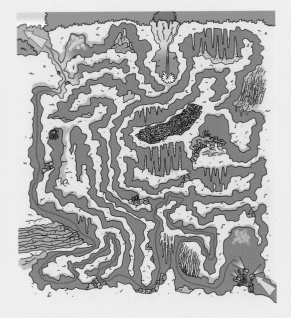

36-37 Southern Tip

42-43 Salty Scramble

44-45   Lost City

46-47   Desert Drawings

48-49   Party Time

50-51   Rainforest Ramble

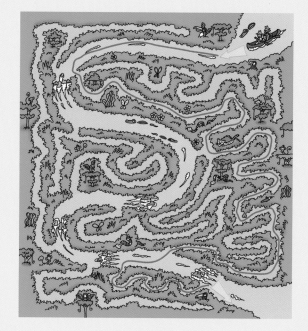

52-53 Island Adventure

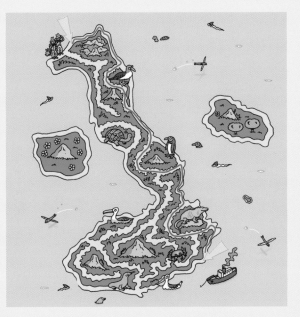

58-59 Lazy River

56-57 History Trek

60-61 Ocean Explorers

62-63 The Big Apple

64-65 Niagara Falls

66-67 Tornado Alley

68-69 Cherokee Trail

70-71   Rocky Road

74-75   Dinosaur Dig

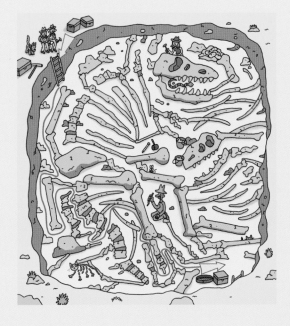

72-73   Cattle Drive

76-77   The Last Frontier

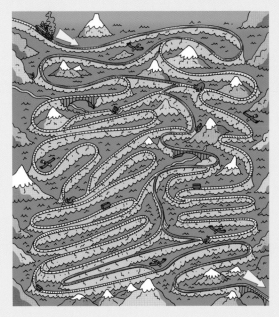

78-79 Island State

82-83 Dragon Dance

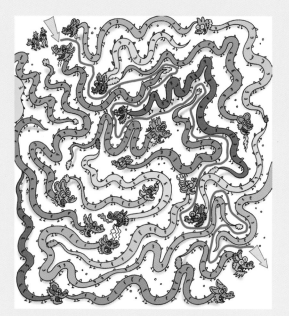

84-85 Great Wall

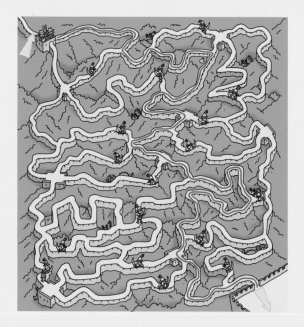

86-87 Sight Seeing

88-89   Man-made Wonders

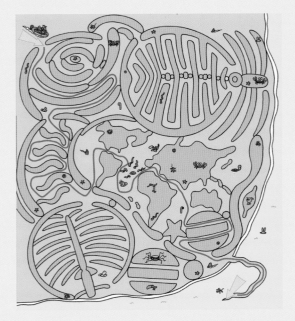

92-93   Come to Cambodia

90-91   Head for Heights

94-95   Rainy Season

96-97   Ring of Fire

102-103   City Sights

100-101   Down Under

104-105   Great Outdoors

106-107 Kangaroo Island

108-109 Tassie Time

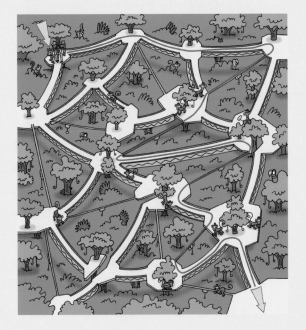

110-111 Kia Ora!

112-113 Extreme Thrills

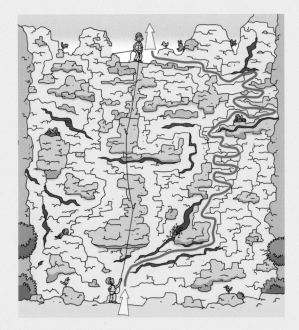

114-115 Journey's End